D1476306

POPE FRANCIS
THE YEAR OF MERCY

POPE FRANCIS
THE YEAR OF MERCY

edited by
Vincenzo Sansonetti

introduction by
Archbishop Rino Fisichella

RIZZOLI
NEW YORK

New York · Paris · London · Milan

Mercy is
an Encounter

by Archbishop Rino Fisichella*

On March 13, 2015, on the second anniversary of his election to the papal cathedra, Pope Francis announced an extraordinary Jubilee of Mercy. The unexpected announcement caught everyone by surprise; yet, the fact that he wanted a Jubilee Year dedicated to mercy shouldn't completely shock us. In fact, from his first *Angelus* on March 17, 2013, his attention has been focused on mercy, which he defined right away as the "foundation of faith." Over the last two years, Bergoglio has made constant references to mercy, both in his actions and in his writings, culminating in the Bull of Indiction of the Holy Year, *Misericordiae vultus*.

Mercy is indeed the heart of the Christian message and the very essence of God. Looking to Sacred Scripture, the *Psalms* stand out. They reflect the life of every man and woman: birth and death, the sufferings

* *President of the Pontifical Council for the Promotion of the New Evangelization*

of sickness and the pain of abandonment, war and peace, solitude and the search for God. They are also more broadly a reflection of the cosmos, of the plight of Israel and salvation history. The *Psalms* are the voice of God that becomes the prayer of men who place themselves in his presence, knowing they need his love. The Psalter expresses the grandeur of divine action with great clarity: "[He] pardons all your sins, and heals all your ills, [He] redeems your life from the pit, and crowns you with mercy and compassion" (Ps 103:3–4).

The person of Jesus is the culmination and the fulfillment of the Father's merciful action: "Everything in him speaks of mercy. Nothing in him is devoid of compassion" (*Misericordiae vultus*, 8). Pope Francis reminds us that mercy is not an abstract idea, but rather a person to encounter, a face to contemplate. It's precisely in fixing our gaze on Jesus and his face filled with mercy that we can begin to understand the Love of the Trinity. One way Jesus manifests the Father's mercy is in his teachings, for example in his parables, in which he presents a God who is full of joy, especially when he forgives. Specifically, the Pope directs our attention to the parable of the lost sheep, the missing coin, and of the father with his two sons (cfr Lk 15:1–32).

Over the course of history, mercy has been reflected and lived out in the lives of many saints who have made it their one aim in life, despite the difficult situations in which they found themselves in life. To these we must add the hundreds of thousands of simple men and women whose "names are written in the book of life" (Rev 13:8), who brought Christ's teaching to life through their daily faithfulness to the Gospel, putting the various works of mercy into practice. The words of Bergoglio at the end of the Bull, and their deep significance, come to mind, "Our prayer also extends to the saints and blessed ones who made divine mercy their mission in life" (*Misericordiae vultus*, 24).

Pope Francis' invocation of an extraordinary Holy Year, then, is a sign of the attention and of the witness that he offers daily to the Church and to the world. Now, the call is extended to everyone: "We need constantly to contemplate the mystery of mercy. It is a wellspring of joy, serenity, and peace. Our salvation depends on it. Mercy: the word reveals the very mystery of the Most Holy Trinity. Mercy: the ultimate and supreme act by which God comes to meet us. Mercy: the fundamental law that dwells in the heart of every person who looks sincerely into the eyes of his brothers and sisters on the path of life. Mercy: the bridge that connects God and man, opening our hearts to the hope of being loved forever despite our sinfulness" (*Misericordiae vultus*, 2).

The Jubilee is an extraordinary occasion to give strength and vigor to that which makes up the ordinary life of the Church and of every Christian: living as a sign of God's nearness and his tenderness. It's an immense, demanding challenge, especially in the cultural context of our day, unfortunately characterized so often by violence and oppression. The Pontiff calls the Church's attention back to this, reminding her of her mission: "May the Church echo the word of God that resounds strong and clear as a message and a sign of pardon, strength, aid, and love. May she never tire of extending mercy, and be ever patient in offering compassion and comfort. May the Church become the voice of every man and woman, and repeat confidently without end: 'Be mindful of your mercy, O Lord, and your steadfast love, for they have been from of old' (Ps 25:6)," (*Misericordiae vultus*, 25).

September 8, 2015
(Feast of the Nativity of the Blessed Virgin Mary)

Pope Francis' Jubilee

by Vincenzo Sansonetti

Mercy is the heart being moved by the material and spiritual poverty of others; an attribute that is human and, first and foremost, divine. It has always been a constant in the life of Jorge Mario Bergoglio, who has, since his childhood, felt the loving presence of God's mercy in a particularly profound way in his life. On the following pages—in the format already used in *Francis: The People's Pope*, and *Pope Francis and the Virgin Mary* (both published by Rizzoli)—we have selected an extensive series of quotes from Pope Francis on the topic of mercy, taken for the most part from the Apostolic Exhortation *Evangelii Gaudium* and from *Misericordiae vultus*, the Bull of Indiction of the Extraordinary Jubilee of Mercy, which will begin on December 8, 2015 (the Solemnity of the Immaculate Conception) and close on November 20, 2016 (the Feast of Christ the King). The quotes are in chronological order with titles composed by the editor, coupled with images that document the breadth and openness of the Holy Father's humanity. Many of the images were taken during his visit on March 21, 2015 to Naples, where he visited Caravaggio's splendid painting, *The Seven Works of Mercy*, a copy of which you can find in this book. We have also included the calendar for the Jubilee Year and the special prayer composed by Pope Francis for the occasion.

11

The Works of Mercy

—⟫◆⟪—

It is my burning desire that, during this Jubilee, the Christian people may reflect on the corporal and spiritual works of mercy. It will be a way to reawaken our conscience, too often grown dull in the face of poverty. And let us enter more deeply into the heart of the Gospel where the poor have a special experience of God's mercy. Jesus introduces us to these works of mercy in his preaching so that we can know whether or not we are living as his disciples. Let us rediscover these *corporal works of mercy*: to feed the hungry, give drink to the thirsty, clothe the naked, welcome the stranger, heal the sick, visit the imprisoned, and bury the dead. And let us not forget the *spiritual works of mercy*: to counsel the doubtful, instruct the ignorant, admonish sinners, comfort the afflicted, forgive offenses, bear patiently those who do us ill, and pray for the living and the dead.

Misericordiae Vultus, *Bull of Indiction*
of the Extraordinary Jubilee of Mercy, April 11, 2015

—⟫◆⟪—

Tenaciousness

The Lord never tires of forgiving: never! It is we who tire of asking his forgiveness. Let us ask for the grace not to tire of asking forgiveness, because he never tires of forgiving. Let us ask for this grace.

Homily of the Mass at St. Anna in the Vatican, March 17, 2013

Patience

God's face is the face of a merciful father who is always patient. Have you thought about God's patience, the patience he has with each one of us? That is his mercy. He always has patience, patience with us, he understands us, he waits for us, he does not tire of forgiving us if we are able to return to him with a contrite heart.

Angelus, *March 17, 2013*

Tenderness

Caring and protecting demand goodness, and call for a certain tenderness. In the Gospels, St. Joseph appears as a strong and courageous man, a working man, yet in his heart we see great tenderness, which is not the virtue of the weak but rather a sign of strength of spirit and a capacity for concern, for compassion, for genuine openness to others, for love. We must not be afraid of goodness, of tenderness!

Homily of the Mass for the Beginning of the Petrine Ministry,
St. Peter's Square, March 19, 2013

Service

True power is service. The Pope must serve all people, especially the poor, the weak, the vulnerable.

Tweet, March 19, 2013

Understanding

Jesus has awakened great hopes, especially in the hearts of the simple, the humble, the poor, the forgotten, those who do not matter in the eyes of the world. He understands human suffering, he has shown the face of God's mercy, and he has bent down to heal body and soul. This is Jesus. This is his heart which looks to all of us, to our sicknesses, to our sins.

Homily of Palm Sunday and of the Passion of Our Lord,
St. Peter's Square, March 24, 2013

Gratuitousness

God thinks like the Samaritan who did not pass by the unfortunate man, pitying him or looking at him from the other side of the road, but helped him without asking for anything in return; without asking whether he was a Jew, a pagan or a Samaritan, whether he was rich or poor: he asked for nothing. He went to help him: God is like this. God thinks like the shepherd who lays down his life in order to defend and save his sheep.

First General Audience, March 27, 2013

Trust

Together let us pray to the Virgin Mary that she help us, Bishop and People, to walk in faith and charity, ever trusting in the Lord's mercy: he always awaits us, loves us, has pardoned us with his Blood and pardons us every time we go to him to ask his forgiveness. Let us trust in his mercy!

Regina Coeli, *April 7, 2013*

Last Judgement

May looking at the Last Judgement never frighten us: rather, may it impel us to live better in the present. God offers us this time with mercy and patience so that we may learn every day to recognize him in the poor and in the lowly. Let us strive for goodness and be watchful in prayer and in love. May the Lord, at the end of our lives and at the end of history, be able to recognize us as good and faithful servants.

General Audience, April 24, 2013

Crisis

At this time of crisis it is important not to become closed in on oneself, but rather to be open and attentive toward others.

Tweet, April 24, 2013

Acts

How marvelous it would be if, at the end of the day, each of us could say: today I have performed an act of charity toward others!

Tweet, April 29, 2013

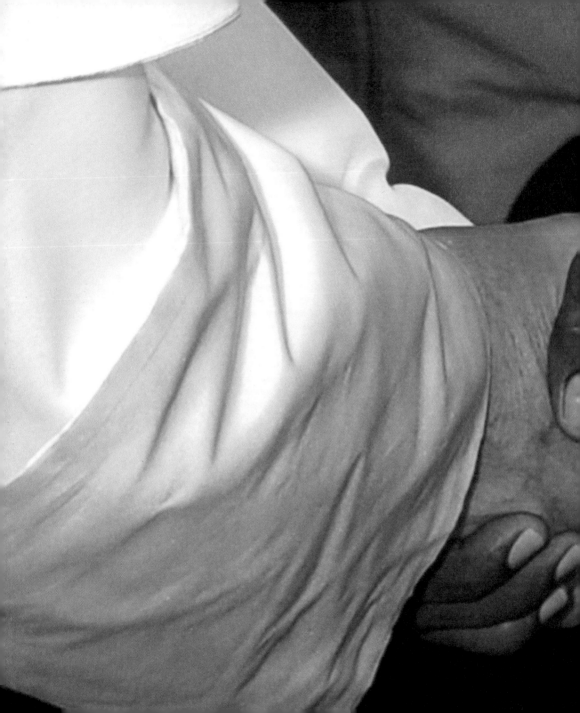

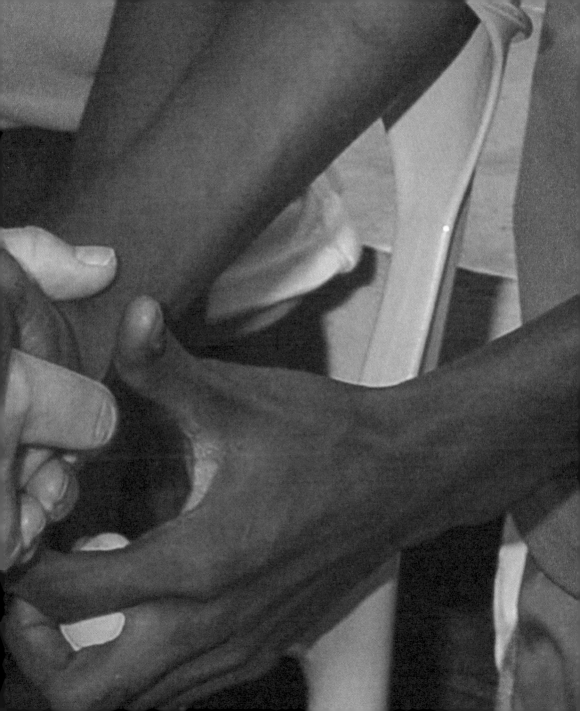

Holy Spirit

The Holy Spirit brings to our hearts a most precious gift: profound
trust in God's love and mercy.

Tweet, May 9, 2013

Openness

When the Church is closed, she falls sick. Think of a room that has been closed for a year. When you go into it there is a damp smell, many things are wrong with it. A Church closed in on herself is the same, a sick Church. The Church must step outside herself. To go where? To the outskirts of existence, whatever they may be.

Vigil of Pentecost with the Ecclesial Movements and the Associations, May 18, 2013

Encounter

We must create a "culture of encounter," a culture of friendship, a culture in which we find brothers and sisters, in which we can also speak with those who think differently, as well as those who hold other beliefs, who do not have the same faith. They all have something in common with us: they are images of God, they are children of God, going out to meet everyone.

Vigil of Pentecost with the Ecclesial Movements and the Associations, May 18, 2013

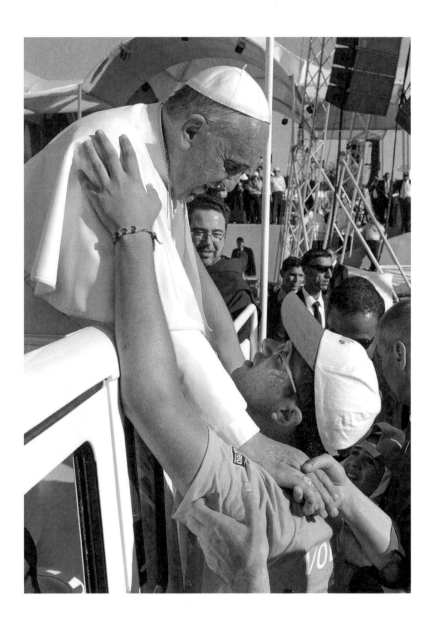

Love

To love God and our neighbor is not something abstract, but profoundly concrete: it means seeing in every person the face of the Lord to be served, to serve him concretely.

Visit at the Homeless Shelter "Dono di Maria," in the Vatican, May 21, 2013

Wounds

As the Church we should remember that in tending the wounds of refugees, evacuees, and the victims of trafficking, we are putting into practice the commandment of love that Jesus bequeathed to us when he identified with the foreigner, with those who are suffering, with all the innocent victims of violence and exploitation.

To the Plenary Assembly of the Pontifical Council for the Pastoral Care of Migrants and Itinerant People, May 24, 2013

Church

The Church is born from the supreme act of love on the Cross, from Jesus' open side. The Church is a family where we love and are loved.

Tweet, May 29, 2013

Worldliness

The world tells us to seek success, power, and money; God tells us to seek humility, service, and love.

Tweet, June 2, 2013

Waste

Consumerism has accustomed us to waste. But throwing food away is like stealing it from the poor and hungry.

Tweet, June 7, 2013

Hope

Let the Church always be a place of mercy and hope, where everyone is welcomed, loved, and forgiven.

Tweet, June 16, 2013

Suffering

If we have found in Jesus meaning for our own lives, we cannot be indifferent to those who are suffering and sad.

Tweet, June 22, 2013

Treasures

Charity, patience, and tenderness are very beautiful gifts. If you have them, you want to share them with others.

Tweet, June 26, 2013

Indifference

Has any one of us wept because of this situation and others like it? Has any one of us grieved for the death of these brothers and sisters? Has any one of us wept for these persons who were on the boat? For the young mothers carrying their babies? For these men who were looking for a means of supporting their families? We are a society that has forgotten how to weep, how to experience compassion— "suffering with" others: the globalization of indifference has taken from us the ability to weep!

Homily of the Mass at Lampedusa, July 8, 2013

Embrace

We pray for a heart that will embrace immigrants. God will judge us upon how we have treated the most needy.

Tweet, July 8, 2013

Charity

Prayer, humility, and charity toward all are essential in the Christian life: they are the way to holiness.

Tweet, July 16, 2013

Selfishness

We all have to learn to embrace the one in need, as St. Francis did. There are so many situations in Brazil, and throughout the world, that require attention, care, and love, like the fight against chemical dependency. Often, instead, it is selfishness that prevails in our society. How many "dealers of death" there are that follow the logic of power and money at any cost! The scourge of drug-trafficking, that favors violence and sows the seeds of suffering and death, requires of society as a whole an act of courage. A reduction in the spread and influence of drug addiction will not be achieved by a liberalization of drug use, as is currently being proposed in various parts of Latin America. [...] We all need to look upon one another with the loving eyes of Christ.

At the St. Francis of Assisi Hospital of Rio de Janeiro, July 24, 2013

Greatness

The measure of the greatness of a society is found in the way it treats those most in need, those who have nothing apart from their poverty.

Tweet, July 25, 2013

Hunger

We cannot sleep peacefully while babies are dying of hunger and the elderly are without medical assistance.

Tweet, August 17, 2013

Salvation

Jesus is the gate opening up to salvation, a gate open to everyone.

Tweet, August 27, 2013

Happiness

Seeking happiness in material things is a sure way of being unhappy.

Tweet, September 15, 2013

Courage

True charity requires courage: let us overcome the fear of getting our hands dirty so as to help those in need.

Tweet, September 21, 2013

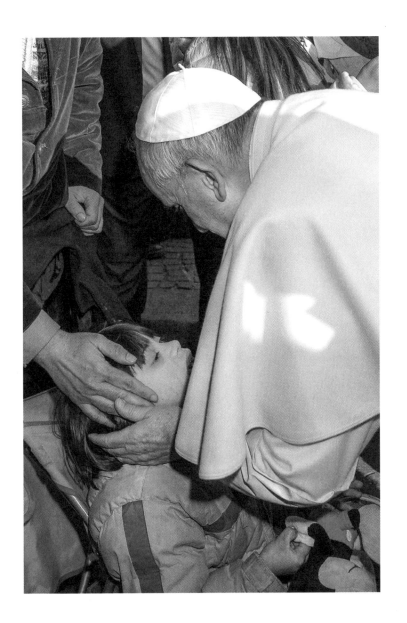

Reflection

We have come together to encounter the gaze of Mary, since there, as it were, is reflected the gaze of the Father, who made her the Mother of God, and the gaze of the Son on the Cross, who made her our Mother. It is with that gaze that Mary watches us today. We need her tender gaze, her maternal gaze, which knows us better than anyone else, her gaze full of compassion and care. Mary, today we want to tell you: Mother grant us your gaze! Your gaze leads us to God, your gaze is a gift of the good Father who waits for us at every turn of our path, it is a gift of Jesus Christ on the Cross, who takes upon himself our sufferings, our struggles, our sin.

Homily of the Mass at the Shrine of Our Lady
of Bonaria (Cagliari), September 22, 2013

Welcome

The gaze of Our Lady helps us to look at one another as brothers and sisters. Let us look upon one another in a more fraternal way! Mary teaches us to have that gaze which strives to welcome, to accompany and to protect. Let us learn to look at one another beneath Mary's maternal gaze! There are people whom we instinctively consider less and who instead are in greater need: the most abandoned, the sick, those who have nothing to live on, those who do not know Jesus, youth who find themselves in difficulty, young people who cannot find work. Let us not be afraid to go out and to look upon our brothers and sisters with Our Lady's gaze. She invites us to be true brothers and sisters.

*Homily of the Mass at the Shrine of Our Lady
of Bonaria (Cagliari), September 22, 2013*

Power

Mercy is the true power that can save humanity and the world from sin and evil.

Tweet, October 7, 2013

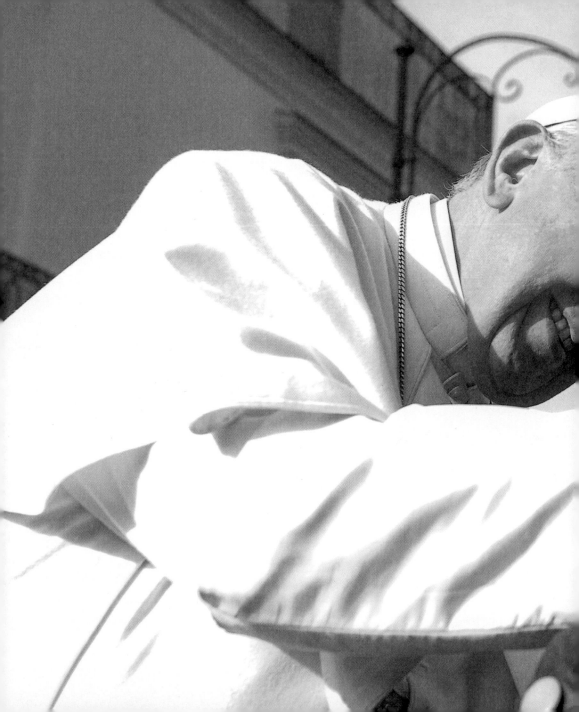

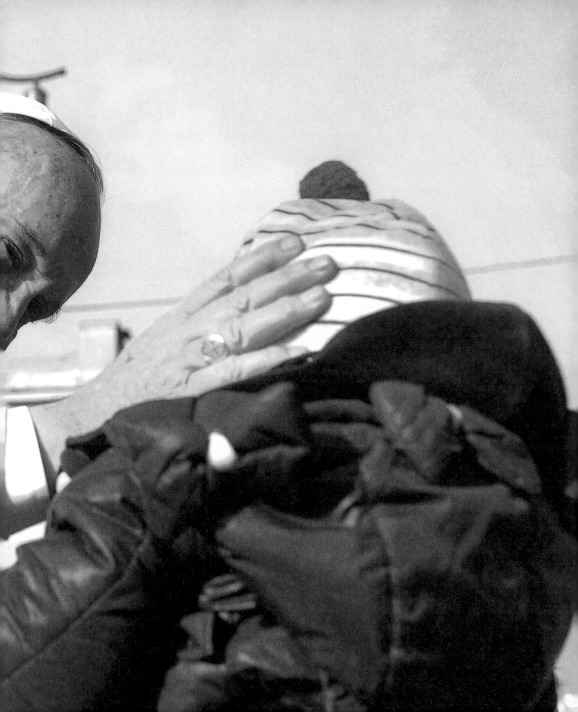

Gaze

At whom is the Virgin Mary looking? She is looking at each and every one of us. And how does she look at us? She looks at us as a Mother, with tenderness, mercy, and love. That was how she gazed at her Son Jesus at all the moments of his life—joyful, luminous, sorrowful, glorious—as we contemplate the mysteries of the Holy Rosary, simply and lovingly.

Video Message for the Vigil "Con Maria oltre la notte"
at the Shrine of Divine Love in Rome, October 12, 2013

Death

The joy of God is not the death of the sinner, but the life of the sinner. […] The joy of God the Father, in fact, is love.

Homily at the Domus Sanctae Marthae, November 7, 2013

Anguish

The great danger in today's world, pervaded as it is by consumerism, is the desolation and anguish born of a complacent yet covetous heart, the feverish pursuit of frivolous pleasures, and a blunted conscience. Whenever our interior life becomes caught up in its own interests and concerns, there is no longer room for others, no place for the poor. God's voice is no longer heard.

Apostolic Exhortation Evangelii Gaudium, *November 24, 2013*

Resurrection

He has forgiven us seventy times seven. Time and time again he bears us on his shoulders. No one can strip us of the dignity bestowed upon us by this boundless and unfailing love. With a tenderness which never disappoints, but is always capable of restoring our joy, he makes it possible for us to lift up our heads and to start anew. Let us not flee from the Resurrection of Jesus, let us never give up, come what will. May nothing inspire more than his life, which impels us onward!

Apostolic Exhortation Evangelii Gaudium, *November 24, 2013*

Goodness

As it expands, goodness takes root and develops. If we wish to lead a dignified and fulfilling life, we have to reach out to others and seek their goodness.

Apostolic Exhortation Evangelii Gaudium, *November 24, 2013*

Announcement

It is vitally important for the Church today to go forth and preach the Gospel to all: to all places, on all occasions, without hesitation, reluctance, or fear. The joy of the Gospel is for all people: no one can be excluded.

Apostolic Exhortation Evangelii Gaudium, *November 24, 2013*

First Step

An evangelizing community [...] has an endless desire to show mercy, the fruit of its own experience of the power of the Father's infinite mercy. Let us try a little harder to take the first step.

Apostolic Exhortation Evangelii Gaudium, *November 24, 2013*

Abasement

Jesus washed the feet of his disciples. The Lord gets involved and he involves his own, as he kneels to wash their feet. [...] An evangelizing community gets involved by word and deed in people's daily lives; it bridges distances, it is willing to abase itself if necessary, and it embraces human life, touching the suffering flesh of Christ in others.

Apostolic Exhortation Evangelii Gaudium, *November 24, 2013*

Virtues

As far as external works are concerned, mercy is the greatest of all the virtues.

Apostolic Exhortation Evangelii Gaudium, *November 24, 2013*

Growth

Without detracting from the evangelical ideal, (people) need to accompany with mercy and patience the eventual stages of personal growth as these progressively occur.

Apostolic Exhortation Evangelii Gaudium, *November 24, 2013*

Confessional

I want to remind priests that the confessional must not be a torture chamber but rather an encounter with the Lord's mercy which spurs us on to do our best.

Apostolic Exhortation Evangelii Gaudium, *November 24, 2013*

Tollbooth

Frequently, we act as arbiters of grace rather than its facilitators. But the Church is not a tollbooth; it is the house of the Father, where there is a place for everyone, with all their problems.

Apostolic Exhortation Evangelii Gaudium, *November 24, 2013*

Poor People

We have to state, without mincing words, that there is an inseparable bond between our faith and the poor. May we never abandon them.

Apostolic Exhortation Evangelii Gaudium, *November 24, 2013*

Comfort Zone

I prefer a Church that is bruised, hurting, and dirty because it has been out on the streets, rather than a Church which is unhealthy from being confined and from clinging to its own security. I do not want a Church concerned with being at the center and which then ends by being caught up in a web of obsessions and procedures. If something should rightly disturb us and trouble our consciences, it is the fact that so many of our brothers and sisters are living without the strength, light, and consolation born of friendship with Jesus Christ, without a community of faith to support them, without meaning and a goal in life.

Apostolic Exhortation Evangelii Gaudium, *November 24, 2013*

Precariousness

The majority of our contemporaries are barely living from day to day, with dire consequences. A number of diseases are spreading. The hearts of many people are gripped by fear and desperation, even in the so-called rich countries.

Apostolic Exhortation Evangelii Gaudium, *November 24, 2013*

Exclusion

We have created a "throw away" culture which is now spreading. It is no longer simply about exploitation and oppression, but something new. Exclusion ultimately has to do with what it means to be a part of the society in which we live [...]. The excluded are not the "exploited" but the outcasts, the "leftovers."

Apostolic Exhortation Evangelii Gaudium, *November 24, 2013*

Solidarity

The rich must help, respect, and promote the poor. I exhort you to generous solidarity and to the return of economics and finance to an ethical approach which favors human beings.

Apostolic Exhortation Evangelii Gaudium, *November 24, 2013*

Appearance

In the prevailing culture, priority is given to the outward, the immediate, the visible, the quick, the superficial, and the provisional. What is real gives way to appearances. In many countries globalization has meant a hastened deterioration of their own cultural roots and the invasion of ways of thinking and acting proper to other cultures that are economically advanced but ethically debilitated.

Apostolic Exhortation Evangelii Gaudium, *November 24, 2013*

Individualism

The individualism of our postmodern and globalized era favors a lifestyle which weakens the development and stability of personal relationships and distorts family bonds.

Apostolic Exhortation Evangelii Gaudium, *November 24, 2013*

Cities

We need to look at our cities with a contemplative gaze, a gaze of faith that sees God dwelling in their homes, in their streets and squares.

Apostolic Exhortation Evangelii Gaudium, *November 24, 2013*

Examples

How many Christians are giving their lives in love? They help so many people to be healed or to die in peace in makeshift hospitals. They are present to those enslaved by different addictions in the poorest places on earth.

Apostolic Exhortation Evangelii Gaudium, *November 24, 2013*

Excuses

The evils of our world—and those of the Church—must not be excuses for diminishing our commitment and our fervor. Let us look upon them as challenges which can help us to grow. With the eyes of faith, we can see the light which the Holy Spirit always radiates in the midst of darkness.

Apostolic Exhortation Evangelii Gaudium, *November 24, 2013*

Desert

In the desert we rediscover the value of what is essential for living; thus in today's world there are innumerable signs, often expressed implicitly or negatively, of the thirst for God, for the ultimate meaning of life.

Apostolic Exhortation Evangelii Gaudium, *November 24, 2013*

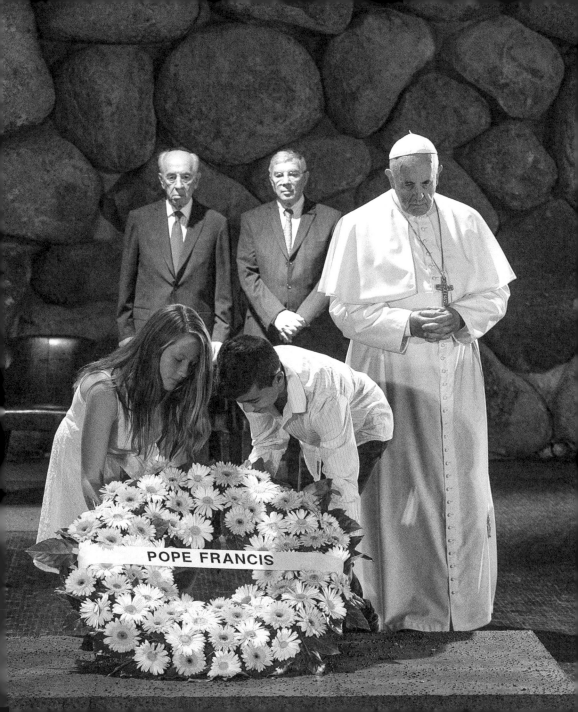

Gift

True faith in the incarnate Son of God is inseparable from self-giving, from membership in the community, from service, from reconciliation with others.

Apostolic Exhortation Evangelii Gaudium, *November 24, 2013*

Witness

I especially ask Christians in communities throughout the world to offer a radiant and attractive witness of fraternal communion. Let everyone admire how you care for one another, and how you encourage and accompany one another: "By this everyone will know that you are my disciples, if you have love for one another" (Jn 13:35).

Apostolic Exhortation Evangelii Gaudium, *November 24, 2013*

Generations

The elderly bring with them memory and the wisdom of experience, which warns us not to foolishly repeat our past mistakes. Young people call us to renewed and expansive hope, for they represent new directions for humanity and open us up to the future, lest we cling to a nostalgia for structures and customs which are no longer life-giving in today's world.

Apostolic Exhortation Evangelii Gaudium, *November 24, 2013*

Preaching

There is a kind of preaching which falls to each of us as a daily responsibility. It has to do with bringing the Gospel to the people we meet, whether they be our neighbors or complete strangers.

Apostolic Exhortation Evangelii Gaudium, *November 24, 2013*

Diversity

Differences between persons and communities can sometimes prove uncomfortable, but the Holy Spirit, who is the source of that diversity, can bring forth something good from all things and turn it into [...] means of evangelization. Diversity must always be reconciled by the help of the Holy Spirit; he alone can raise up diversity, plurality, and multiplicity while at the same time bringing about unity.

Apostolic Exhortation Evangelii Gaudium, *November 24, 2013*

Beauty

Proclaiming Christ means showing that to believe in and to follow him is not only something right and true, but also something beautiful, capable of filling life with new splendor and profound joy, even in the midst of difficulties. Every expression of true beauty can thus be acknowledged as a path leading to an encounter with the Lord Jesus.

Apostolic Exhortation Evangelii Gaudium, *November 24, 2013*

Closeness

In a culture paradoxically suffering from anonymity and at the same time obsessed with the details of other people's lives, shamelessly given over to morbid curiosity, the Church must look more closely and sympathetically at others whenever necessary.

Apostolic Exhortation Evangelii Gaudium, *November 24, 2013*

Social Commitment

No one can demand that religion should be relegated to the inner sanctum of personal life, without influence on societal and national life, without concern for the soundness of civil institutions, without a right to offer an opinion on events affecting society. Who would claim to lock up in a church and silence the message of St. Francis of Assisi or Blessed Teresa of Calcutta?

Apostolic Exhortation Evangelii Gaudium, *November 24, 2013*

Cry

Each individual Christian and every community is called to be an instrument of God for the liberation and promotion of the poor, and for enabling them to be fully a part of society. This demands that we be docile and attentive to the cry of the poor and to come to their aid.

Apostolic Exhortation Evangelii Gaudium, *November 24, 2013*

Dignity

We must never forget that the planet belongs to all mankind and is meant for all mankind; the mere fact that some people are born in places with fewer resources or less development does not justify the fact that they are living with less dignity.

Apostolic Exhortation Evangelii Gaudium, *November 24, 2013*

Vulnerability

It is essential to draw near to new forms of poverty and vulnerability, in which we are called to recognize the suffering Christ [...]. The homeless, the addicted, refugees, indigenous peoples, the elderly who are increasingly isolated and abandoned.

Apostolic Exhortation Evangelii Gaudium, *November 24, 2013*

Integration

How beautiful are those cities that overcome paralyzing mistrust, integrate those who are different, and make this very integration a new factor of development! How attractive are those cities which, even in their architectural design, are full of spaces which connect, relate, and favor the recognition of others!

Apostolic Exhortation Evangelii Gaudium, *November 24, 2013*

Unborn Life

Among the vulnerable for whom the Church wishes to care with particular love and concern are unborn children, the most defenseless and innocent among us. Nowadays efforts are made to deny them their human dignity and to do with them whatever one pleases, taking their lives and passing laws preventing anyone from standing in the way of this.

Apostolic Exhortation Evangelii Gaudium, *November 24, 2013*

Dialogue

In her dialogue with the state and with society, the Church does not have solutions for every particular issue. Together with the various sectors of society, she supports those programs which best respond to the dignity of each person and the common good. In doing this, she proposes in a clear way the fundamental values of human life.

Apostolic Exhortation Evangelii Gaudium, *November 24, 2013*

Evangelization

Mystical notions without a solid social and missionary outreach are of no help to evangelization, nor are dissertations or social or pastoral practices which lack a spirituality which can change hearts.

Apostolic Exhortation Evangelii Gaudium, *November 24, 2013*

Prayer

What is needed is the ability to cultivate an interior space which can give a Christian meaning to commitment and activity.

Apostolic Exhortation Evangelii Gaudium, *November 24, 2013*

Memory

We do well to keep in mind the early Christians and our many brothers and sisters throughout history who were filled with joy, unflagging courage, and zeal in proclaiming the Gospel.

Apostolic Exhortation Evangelii Gaudium, *November 24, 2013*

Jesus

Jesus' whole life, his way of dealing with the poor, his actions, his integrity, his simple daily acts of generosity, and finally his complete self-giving, is precious and reveals the mystery of his divine life.

Apostolic Exhortation Evangelii Gaudium, *November 24, 2013*

Imitation

In union with Jesus, we seek what he seeks and we love what he loves. In the end, what we are seeking is the glory of the Father [...] which Jesus sought at every moment of his life.

Apostolic Exhortation Evangelii Gaudium, *November 24, 2013*

Distance

Sometimes we are tempted to be that kind of Christian who keeps the Lord's wounds at arm's length. Yet Jesus wants us to touch human misery, to touch the suffering flesh of others. He hopes that we will stop looking for those personal or communal niches which shelter us from the maelstrom of human misfortune and instead enter into the reality of other people's lives.

Apostolic Exhortation Evangelii Gaudium, November 24, 2013

Creation

If we are to share our lives with others and generously give of ourselves, we also have to realize that every person is worthy of our giving. Not for their physical appearance, their abilities, their language, their way of thinking, or for any satisfaction that we might receive, but rather because they are God's handiwork, his creation.

Apostolic Exhortation Evangelii Gaudium, *November 24, 2013*

Darkness

Often it seems that God does not exist: all around us we see persistent injustice, evil, indifference, and cruelty. But it is also true that in the midst of darkness something new always springs to life and sooner or later produces fruit. On razed land life breaks through, stubbornly yet invincibly.

Apostolic Exhortation Evangelii Gaudium, *November 24, 2013*

Seed

Let us believe the Gospel when it tells us that the Kingdom of God is already present in this world and is growing, here and there, and in different ways: like the small seed which grows into a great tree.

Apostolic Exhortation Evangelii Gaudium, *November 24, 2013*

Mary

Mary was able to turn a stable into a home for Jesus, with poor swaddling clothes and an abundance of love. She is the handmaid of the Father who sings his praises. She is the friend who is ever concerned that wine not be lacking in our lives. She is the woman whose heart was pierced by a sword and who understands all our pain. As mother of all, she is a sign of hope for people suffering the birth pangs of justice.

Apostolic Exhortation Evangelii Gaudium, *November 24, 2013*

Samaritans

If we see someone who needs help, do we stop? There is so much suffering and poverty, and a great need for good Samaritans.

Tweet, December 9, 2013

Table

Let us leave a spare place at our table: a place for those who lack the basics, who are alone.

Tweet, January 7, 2014

Grace

Mercy brings us peace! Let us always remember: who am I to judge? To be ashamed of oneself and to open and expand one's heart, may the Lord give us this grace!

Homily at the Domus Sanctae Marthae, *March 17, 2014*

Without Limit

Jesus is never far from us sinners. He wants to pour out on us, without limit, all of his mercy.

Tweet, March 24, 2014

Caress

The mercy of God: it is a great light of love, of tenderness. God doesn't forgive with a decree but with a caress. He forgives by caressing the wounds caused by our sins.

Homily at the Domus Sanctae Marthae, *April 7, 2014*

Gospel

Let us read the Gospel, a small section each day. This way we will
learn what is most essential in our lives: love and mercy.

Tweet, May 13, 2014

Message

It is by God's mercy that we are saved. May we never tire of spreading this joyful message to the world.

Tweet, August 17, 2014

Joy

May we help people to discover the joy of the Christian message: a message of love and mercy.

Tweet, October 28, 2014

Exploitation

My hope is that man's exploitation of man may be overcome. This kind of exploitation is a social plague which demeans interpersonal relationships and impedes a life of communion based on respect, justice, and charity.

Angelus, *January 4, 2015*

Immigrants

We must make our immigrant brothers and sisters feel that they are citizens, that they are like us, children of God, that they are immigrants like us, because we are all immigrants moving toward another homeland, and perhaps we will all arrive there. And no one will get lost on the way! We are all immigrants, children of God who has placed us all on a journey.

Meeting with the People of the Scampia Neighborhood
during the Journey to Naples, March 21, 2015

Providence

Nothing can ever separate us from God's love, not even prison bars! [...] In the midst of so many problems, even serious ones, we cannot lose our hope in God's infinite mercy and his providence.

Lunch with the Inmates of Poggioreale
during the Journey to Naples, March 21, 2015

The Sick

One can approach illness only in the spirit of faith. We can draw near to a sick man, woman, boy or girl, only if we look to Him who took all of our sickness upon Himself, if we become accustomed to looking at Christ Crucified.

*Meeting with the Sick at the Basilica del Gesù Nuovo
during the Journey to Naples, March 21, 2015*

Discard

This is how our society is. How many people prefer to discard children and comfort themselves with a dog or cat! Children are discarded, the elderly are discarded because we leave them on their own.

Meeting with the Young People and the Families during the Journey to Naples, March 21, 2015

Mystery

We need constantly to contemplate the mystery of mercy. It is a wellspring of joy, serenity, and peace. Our salvation depends on it. Mercy: the word reveals the very mystery of the Most Holy Trinity. Mercy: the ultimate and supreme act by which God comes to meet us. Mercy: the fundamental law that dwells in the heart of every person who looks sincerely into the eyes of his brothers and sisters on the path of life. Mercy: the bridge that connects God and man, opening our hearts to the hope of being loved forever despite our sinfulness.

Misericordiae Vultus, *Bull of Indiction
of the Extraordinary Jubilee of Mercy, April 11, 2015*

Sin

When faced with the gravity of sin, God responds with the fullness of mercy. Mercy will always be greater than any sin, and no one can place limits on the love of God who is always ready to forgive.

Misericordiae Vultus, *Bull of Indiction
of the Extraordinary Jubilee of Mercy, April 11, 2015*

Balm

How much I desire that the year to come will be steeped in mercy, so that we can go out to every man and woman, bringing the goodness and tenderness of God! May the balm of mercy reach everyone, both believers and those far away, as a sign that the Kingdom of God is already present in our midst!

Misericordiae Vultus, *Bull of Indiction*
of the Extraordinary Jubilee of Mercy, April 11, 2015

Prevail

"Patient and merciful." These words often go together in the Old Testament to describe God's nature. His being merciful is concretely demonstrated in his many actions throughout the history of salvation where his goodness prevails over punishment and destruction.

Misericordiae Vultus, *Bull of Indiction of the Extraordinary Jubilee of Mercy, April 11, 2015*

Poignancy

The mercy of God is not an abstract idea, but a concrete reality with which he reveals his love as of that of a father or a mother, moved to the very depths out of love for their child.

Misericordiae Vultus, *Bull of Indiction*
of the Extraordinary Jubilee of Mercy, April 11, 2015

Compassion

Jesus, seeing the crowds of people who followed him, realized that they were tired and exhausted, lost and without a guide, and he felt deep compassion for them.

Misericordiae Vultus, *Bull of Indiction of the Extraordinary Jubilee of Mercy, April 11, 2015*

Heart

What moved Jesus in all of these situations was nothing other than mercy, with which he read the hearts of those he encountered and responded to their deepest need.

Misericordiae Vultus, *Bull of Indiction of the Extraordinary Jubilee of Mercy, April 11, 2015*

Offenses

Jesus affirms that mercy is not only an action of the Father, it becomes a criterion for ascertaining who his true children are. In short, we are called to show mercy because mercy has first been shown to us. Pardoning offenses becomes the clearest expression of merciful love, and for us Christians it is an imperative from which we cannot excuse ourselves. At times how hard it seems to forgive! And yet pardon is the instrument placed into our fragile hands to attain serenity of heart. To let go of anger, wrath, violence, and revenge is a necessary condition to living joyfully.

Misericordiae Vultus, *Bull of Indiction*
of the Extraordinary Jubilee of Mercy, April 11, 2015

Concreteness

In Sacred Scripture, mercy is a key word that indicates God's action toward us. He does not limit himself merely to affirming his love, but makes it visible and tangible. Love, after all, can never be just an abstraction. By its very nature, it indicates something concrete: intentions, attitudes, and behaviors that are shown in daily living.

Misericordiae Vultus, *Bull of Indiction*
of the Extraordinary Jubilee of Mercy, April 11, 2015

Responsibility

The mercy of God is his loving concern for each one of us. He feels responsible; that is, he desires our wellbeing and he wants to see us happy, full of joy, and peaceful. This is the path which the merciful love of Christians must also travel. As the Father loves, so do his children. Just as he is merciful, so we are called to be merciful to each other.

Misericordiae Vultus, *Bull of Indiction*
of the Extraordinary Jubilee of Mercy, April 11, 2015

Credibility

Mercy is the very foundation of the Church's life. All of her pastoral activity should be caught up in the tenderness she makes present to believers; nothing in her preaching and in her witness to the world can be lacking in mercy. The Church's very credibility is seen in how she shows merciful and compassionate love.

Misericordiae Vultus, *Bull of Indiction of the Extraordinary Jubilee of Mercy, April 11, 2015*

Forgiveness

Sad to say, we must admit that the practice of mercy is waning in the wider culture. In some cases the word seems to have dropped out of use. However, without a witness to mercy, life becomes fruitless and sterile, as if sequestered in a barren desert. The time has come for the Church to take up the joyful call to mercy once more.

Misericordiae Vultus, *Bull of Indiction
of the Extraordinary Jubilee of Mercy, April 11, 2015*

Enthusiasm

The theme of mercy needs to be proposed again and again with new enthusiasm and renewed pastoral action. It is absolutely essential for the Church and for the credibility of her message that she herself live and testify to mercy. Her language and her gestures must transmit mercy, so as to touch the hearts of all people and inspire them once more to find the road that leads to the Father.

Misericordiae Vultus, *Bull of Indiction of the Extraordinary Jubilee of Mercy, April 11, 2015*

Truth

The Church's first truth is the love of Christ. The Church makes herself a servant of this love and mediates it to all people: a love that forgives and expresses itself in the gift of oneself. Consequently, wherever the Church is present, the mercy of the Father must be evident.

Misericordiae Vultus, *Bull of Indiction
of the Extraordinary Jubilee of Mercy, April 11, 2015*

Aid

In mercy, we find proof of how God loves us. He gives his entire self, always, freely, asking nothing in return. He comes to our aid whenever we call upon him.

Misericordiae Vultus, *Bull of Indiction of the Extraordinary Jubilee of Mercy, April 11, 2015*

Friendship

Let us open our eyes and see the misery of the world, the wounds of our brothers and sisters who are denied their dignity, and let us recognize that we are compelled to heed their cry for help! May we reach out to them and support them so they can feel the warmth of our presence, our friendship, and our fraternity!

Misericordiae Vultus, *Bull of Indiction
of the Extraordinary Jubilee of Mercy, April 11, 2015*

Signs

Confessors are authentic signs of the Father's mercy. We do not become good confessors automatically. We become good confessors when, above all, we allow ourselves to be penitents in search of his mercy. Let us never forget that to be confessors means to participate in the very mission of Jesus, to be a concrete sign of the constancy of divine love that pardons and saves.

Misericordiae Vultus, *Bull of Indiction of the Extraordinary Jubilee of Mercy, April 11, 2015*

Conversion

I direct this invitation to conversion even more fervently to those whose behavior distances them from the grace of God. I particularly have in mind men and women belonging to criminal organizations of any kind. For their own good, I beg them to change their lives. I ask them this in the name of the Son of God who, though rejecting sin, never rejected the sinner.

Misericordiae Vultus, *Bull of Indiction of the Extraordinary Jubilee of Mercy, April 11, 2015*

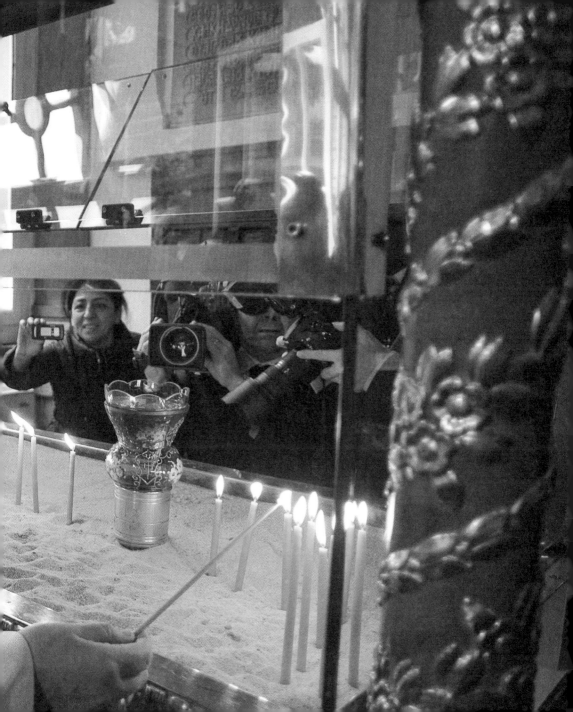

Corruption

Corruption prevents us from looking to the future with hope, because its tyrannical greed shatters the plans of the weak and tramples upon the poorest of the poor.

Misericordiae Vultus, *Bull of Indiction of the Extraordinary Jubilee of Mercy, April 11, 2015*

Justice

Mercy is not opposed to justice but rather expresses God's way of reaching out to the sinner, offering him a new chance to look at himself, convert, and believe.

Misericordiae Vultus, *Bull of Indiction*
of the Extraordinary Jubilee of Mercy, April 11, 2015

Paying The Price

If God limited himself to only justice, he would cease to be God, and would instead be like human beings who ask merely that the law be respected. But mere justice is not enough [...]. This is why God goes beyond justice with his mercy and forgiveness. Yet this does not mean that justice should be devalued or rendered superfluous. On the contrary: anyone who makes a mistake must pay the price. However, this is just the beginning of conversion, not its end, because one begins to feel the tenderness and mercy of God. God does not deny justice. He rather envelops it and surpasses it with an even greater event in which we experience love as the foundation of true justice.

Misericordiae Vultus, Bull of Indiction
of the Extraordinary Jubilee of Mercy, April 11, 2015

Israel

There is an aspect of mercy that goes beyond the confines of the Church. [...] Israel was the first to receive this revelation which continues in history as the source of an inexhaustible richness meant to be shared with all mankind. [...] The pages of the Old Testament are steeped in mercy, because they narrate the works that the Lord performed in favor of his people at the most trying moments of their history.

Misericordiae Vultus, *Bull of Indiction of the Extraordinary Jubilee of Mercy, April 11, 2015*

Islam

Among the privileged names that Islam attributes to the Creator are "Merciful and Kind." This invocation is often on the lips of faithful Muslims who feel themselves accompanied and sustained by mercy in their daily weakness. They too believe that no one can place a limit on divine mercy because its doors are always open.

Misericordiae Vultus, *Bull of Indiction*
of the Extraordinary Jubilee of Mercy, April 11, 2015

Cross

At the foot of the Cross, Mary, together with John, the disciple of love, witnessed the words of forgiveness spoken by Jesus. This supreme expression of mercy toward those who crucified him show us the point to which the mercy of God can reach.

Misericordiae Vultus, *Bull of Indiction of the Extraordinary Jubilee of Mercy, April 11, 2015*

Faustina Kowalska

Our prayer also extends to the saints and blessed ones who made divine mercy their mission in life. I think especially of the great apostle of mercy, St. Faustina Kowalska. May she, who was called to enter the depths of divine mercy, intercede for us and obtain for us the grace of living and walking always according to the mercy of God and with an unwavering trust in his love.

Misericordiae Vultus, *Bull of Indiction*
of the Extraordinary Jubilee of Mercy, April 11, 2015

Vocation

Being Christian is not an appearance or a social practice, it isn't a makeover for the soul so that it might be a little prettier; it is doing what Jesus did: serving.

Homily at the Domus Sanctae Marthae, April 30, 2015

Jobs

Unemployment takes away dignity, prevents the fullness of human life, and calls for an immediate and vigorous response [...]. Against this global economic system in which man and woman are not at the center: there is an idol, the god of money.

Address to the Italian Christian Workers' Associations (ACLI), for the 70th Anniversary of Its Foundation, May 23, 2015

Riches

Riches are for the common good, for all, and if the Lord grants them to someone, it is for the good of all, not for oneself, not to close within one's heart, which then becomes corrupt and sorrowful.

Homily at the Domus Sanctae Marthae, May 25, 2015

Beatitudes

We need to build up society in the light of the Beatitudes, walking toward the Kingdom with the least among us.

Tweet, June 4, 2015

Enemy

Those whom I looked upon as my enemy really have the same face as I do, the same heart, the same soul. We have the same Father in heaven.

Homily at Koševo Stadium, June 6, 2015

Us

You are a Muslim, you are a Jew, you are Orthodox, you are Catholic...
but we are "us." This is how to make peace. And this distinguishes
your generation, and it is your joy! You are called to great things! A
great vocation: build bridges, not walls.

Meeting with the Young People in Sarajevo, June 6, 2015

Prayer
of Pope Francis for the Jubilee

———⟫◆⟪———

Lord Jesus Christ,
you have taught us to be merciful like the heavenly Father,
and have told us that whoever sees you sees Him.
Show us your face and we will be saved.
Your loving gaze freed Zacchaeus and Matthew
from being enslaved by money;
the adulteress and Magdalene
from seeking happiness only in created things;
made Peter weep after his betrayal,
and assured Paradise to the repentant thief.
Let us hear, as if addressed to each one of us,
the words that you spoke to the Samaritan woman:
"If you knew the gift of God!"

You are the visible face of the invisible Father,
of the God who manifests his power
above all by forgiveness and mercy:

let the Church be your visible face in the world,
its Lord risen and glorified.
You willed that your ministers would also be clothed in weakness
in order that they may feel compassion
for those in ignorance and error:
let everyone who approaches them feel sought after, loved, and
forgiven by God.

Send your Spirit and consecrate every one of us with its anointing,
so that the Jubilee of Mercy may be a year of grace from the Lord,
and your Church, with renewed enthusiasm,
may bring good news to the poor,
proclaim liberty to captives and the oppressed,
and restore sight to the blind.

We ask this through the intercession of Mary, Mother of Mercy,
you who live and reign with the Father and the Holy Spirit
for ever and ever. Amen.

The Seven Works of Mercy (on the opposite page) is the subject of a work by the Italian painter Michelangelo Merisi da Caravaggio, completed between the end of 1606 and the beginning of 1607, and received by those who commissioned it on January 9 of that year. The painting, which is housed in the church of Pio Monte della Misericordia in Naples, depicts in a unique painting "the seven works of corporal mercy."

Jubilee of Mercy
Official Calender

⟫•◆•⟪

December 2015

Tuesday, December 8, 2015
Solemnity of the Immaculate Conception
Opening of the Holy Door of St. Peter's Basilica.

Sunday, December 13, 2015
III Sunday of Advent
Opening of the Holy Door of the Basilica of St. John Lateran
and of St. Paul Outside the Walls, and in the Cathedrals of the world.

January 2016

Friday, January 1, 2016
Solemnity of Mary, the Holy Mother of God
World Day for Peace.
Opening of the Holy Door of the Basilica of Saint Mary Major.

Tuesday, January 19 – Thursday, January 21, 2016
Jubilee for those Engaged in Pilgrimage Work

Monday, January 25, 2016
Feast of the Conversion of St. Paul
Ecumenical Celebration in the Basilica of St. Paul Outside the Walls.
"Jubilee" sign of the Holy Father: witness of the works of mercy.

Tuesday, February 2, 2016
Feast of the Presentation of the Lord and the Day for Consecrated Life
Jubilee for Consecrated Life and the closing of the Year for Consecrated Life.

Wednesday, February 10, 2016
Ash Wednesday
Sending forth of the Missionaries of Mercy, St. Peter's Basilica.

Monday, February 22, 2016
Feast of the Chair of St. Peter
Jubilee for the Roman Curia, for the Governorate and for the
Institutions Connected with the Holy See
"Jubilee" sign of the Holy Father: witness of the works of mercy.

March 2016
Friday, March 4 and Saturday, March 5, 2016
"24 Hours for the Lord" with a penitential liturgy in St. Peter's Basilica
on the afternoon of Friday, March 4.

Sunday, March 20, 2016
Palm Sunday
The diocesan day for youth in Rome.
"Jubilee" sign of the Holy Father: witness of the works of mercy.

April 2016
Sunday, April 3, 2016
Divine Mercy Sunday
Jubilee for those who are devoted to the spirituality of Divine Mercy.

Sunday, April 24, 2016
V Sunday of Easter
Jubilee for young boys and girls (ages 13–16)
To profess the faith and construct a culture of mercy.
"Jubilee" sign of the Holy Father: witness of the works of mercy.

May 2016

Friday, May 27 – Sunday, May 29, 2016
The Solemnity of Corpus Christi in Italy
Jubilee for deacons.

June 2016

Friday, June 3, 2016
Solemnity of the Most Sacred Heart of Jesus
Jubilee for priests.
160 years since the introduction of the Feast by Pius IX in 1856.

Sunday, June 12, 2016
XI Sunday of Ordinary Time
Jubilee for those who are ill and for persons with disabilities.
"Jubilee" sign of the Holy Father: witness of the works of mercy.

July 2016

Tuesday, July 26 – Sunday, July 31, 2016
To conclude on the XVIII Sunday of Ordinary Time
Jubilee for young people.
World Youth Day in Krakow, Poland.

September 2016

Sunday, September 4, 2016
XXIII Sunday of Ordinary Time
Memorial of Blessed Teresa of Calcutta – September 5
Jubilee for workers and volunteers of mercy

Sunday, September 25, 2016
XXVI Sunday of Ordinary Time
Jubilee for catechists

October 2016

Saturday, October 8 and Sunday, October 9, 2016
Saturday and Sunday after the Memorial of Our Lady of the Rosary
Marian Jubilee

November 2016

Tuesday, November 1, 2016
Solemnity of All Saints
Holy Mass celebrated by the Holy Father in memory of the faithful departed.

Sunday, November 6, 2016
XXXII Sunday of Ordinary Time
In St. Peter's Basilica, the Jubilee for prisoners.

Sunday, November 13, 2016
XXXIII Sunday of Ordinary Time
Closing of the Holy Doors in the Basilicas of Rome and in the Dioceses of the world.

Sunday, November 20, 2016
Solemnity of Our Lord Jesus Christ, King of the Universe
Closing of the Holy Door of St. Peter's Basilica and the conclusion of the Jubilee of Mercy.

SOURCE: Pontifical Council for the Promotion of the New Evangelization (www.im.va), a reference for all the news and updates on the Jubilee of Mercy.

Index

First published in the United States of America in 2015 by
Rizzoli International Publications, Inc.
300 Park Avenue South
New York, NY 10010
www.rizzoliusa.com

Originally published in Italian in 2015 by
RCS Libri S.p.A.

Photographs © "L'Osservatore Romano" Photographic Service
except the following:
© Ansa/Osservatore Romano Press Office, pp. 110, 168-169, 182
Courtesy Daria Rescaldani/Ultreya, p. 235
Photo Leemage/UIG via Getty Images, p. 258

Texts © 2015 Libreria Editrice Vaticana, Vatican City

Introductions by Archbishop Rino Fisichella and Vincenzo Sansonetti, translated by Kristin Hurd
Art direction and layout by Ultreya, Milan

2015 2016 2017 2018 / 10 9 8 7 6 5 4 3 2 1

ISBN: 978-0-8478-4910-9

Library of Congress Control Number: 2015945440

Printed in Italy